In Praise of
La Lengua Inside Me

In *La Lengua Inside Me*, Adrian Ernesto Cepeda Spanglish tongue astounds; rolling rhyme, meter, and meaning between the lines and languages and filling the spaces between. Cepeda draws hidden strength from his espejo, his pluma, his literary and artistic heroes, and most importantly, from recuerdos of his mother and father from his childhood, to reveal himself to his readers and actively empower them to find their own strength in heritage, self-love, and creativity.

—**David A. Romero**, Poet and Author of *My Name is Romero*

Adrian Ernesto Cepeda's *La Lengua Inside Me* buzzes, vibrant and alive with curiosity, awe, joy, noticing everything, and speaking in the language of the heart. Potent, poignant, powerful. I feel my own coming of age on the borderlands singing through every line. From Frida Kahlo to Gabriel Garcia Márquez, from la playa to La Dairy Queen in the desert, these poems sing with Latinx joy! Comida, familia, amor. I couldn't ask for more in a poetry collection. A must-read celebration of Latinx heritage and voice.

—**Jenn Givhan**, author of *Landscape with Headless Mama* and *Belly to the Brutal*

A Spanglish Stammer opens a collection of poems. A writer recalls a distant Saturday afternoon from days of boyhood. As a child he asks his father what he is to do with his life? What pursuits are worthy of pride? What he is to become? His father answers to be.

The child dreams in cinema. The child dreams of poetry, of Neruda. Frida awakens the stars. His father agrees with Marquez. A poet's mother speaks to, cleans, repairs glass figurines, bonds with them in ways a poet will not understand until they are long packed away and his mother is gone.

The world of Adrian Ernesto Cepeda is one of instant wonder and delayed revelation. These pages build in momentum and meaning with each successive poem. It is a slow burn towards worlds familiar, unfamiliar and those just now being born.

—**Matt Sedillo**, author of *Mowing Leaves of Grass* and *City on the Second Floor*

LA LENGUA INSIDE *me*

FLOWERSONG
PRESS

poetry by

ADRIAN ERNESTO CEPEDA

FLOWERSONG
PRESS

Acknowledgements

Some poems in this book first appeared in the following publications, sometimes in slightly different form:

Barrio Panther: "For My Lover, Returning to Her Husband," "Waiting at the Gate, for mi Novia, Sept 1998, San Antonio International Airport;" "Bending with blood—Sangre me Futbol;" "Quienes son los enemigos;"

Glass Poetry: Poets Resist: "A Donde Esta mi Mama y Papa?"

Latino Books Review: "What Puro Amor Tastes Like..."

Latinx Lit Mag. "Starry, Starry Light"

Los Angeles Poetry Society's Re-Fleshing Anthology: "I Know This is Muy Dificil"

Lunch Ticket: "Ode to her Unibrow"

Memories of Food Anthology" "Del Taco Bell is Not Poetic"

My Abuela Stories: "Ella era la Silenciosa"

Neon Mariposa Magazine: "Between My Shadow"

Olney Magazine: "Pilgrimage from San Antonio to Corpus Christi"

orangepeel literary magazine: "I Once Saw Frida Kahlo"

The Pangolin Review: "The Secret Muse of Gabriel Garcia Márquez"

Pine Hills Review: "Why Mi Mami Loves You, Rafa Nadal"

Rogue Agent Journal: "Invisible Tan"

Seattle Escribe's proyecto digital Poemas para la cuarentena: "40 Por Ciento"

Sims Library of Poetry's Poem-a Week: "Poetry Journey"

Spectrum Publishing's Scenes of Southern California: A Directory of So Cal Poets: "Con El Mar Behind Me"

Subterranean Blue Poetry's The Beat Poets issue: "I was in total Silencio until…"

Transcendence Magazine: "Ode to Don Jose"

Table of Contents

PART II

PART III

"a poet must write in the language of his childhood"

—Czesław Miłosz

Dedication

La Lengua Inside Me is dedicated to mi esposa Michelle. With her support, love, and belief en mi voz, in mis poemas, y este libro, inspires my ever-evolving poetry career to become a reality. Te Amo, Baby. Thank You for being the first one to hear and read my poems when they have first been brought to life. Gracias for your encouragement and being an integral part of every stage of the creation process. *La Lengua Inside Me* would not exist without you, mi amor.

Gracias Papi, Mami, los abuelitos Bernal y Cepeda, mi familia Rene y Mary, Joe y Chante, cada uno that inspired *La Lengua Inside* este libro de mi poesias.

Millones de gracias to mi FlowerSong Press Familia: Briana Muñoz, Gina Duran, Matt Sedillo, David Romero, Iris De Anda, Luivette Resto, Sonia Gutiérrez, Luis Alberto Urrea, Kai Coggin, Ariel Francisco, Priscilla Celina Suarez, Gris Muñoz for introducing me to FlowerSong Press, Natalie Sierra for your support & championing mi libro and Edward Vidaurre for believing in my work and publishing *La Lengua Inside Me.*

For your inspiration, Thank You: Jenn Givhan, Sandra Cisneros, Ada Limón, Gabriel Garcia Marquez, Frida Kahlo, Perls, Diego Luna, Carlos Fuentes, Juan Gabriel Vasquez, Mario Monteforte Toledo, Vivian Arimany, Anne Sexton, Cristiano Ronaldo, Brian Wilson, Rafael Nadal, The Beatles, Carl Sagan, Vincent van Gogh, Don McLean, Miles Davis, Amy Shimshon-Santo, Tom Waits, A.L. Rascon, John Cusack, Lloyd Dobler, Myriam Gurba, Linda Yvette Chávez + Marvin Lemus and The Morales familia from *Gentefied*, Virginia Woolf, Selena Quintanilla, Jack Kerouac, Allen Ginsberg, William Burroughs, Jimmy Santiago Baca, Pablo Neruda, Jean Paul-Sartre, Carol Rodriguez, Nancy Rehfeld, Faby Ryan, Virginia Bulacio and Jean-Pierre Rueda.

LA LENGUA
INSIDE *me*

Es Verdad

¿Qué estoy
buscando?
Solo saben mi
Poesia.

Gracias, Jean-Paul Sartre

I:

"To gain your own voice, you have to forget about having it heard."

— **Allen Ginsberg**

My stutter es mi acento

When I stammer trying to
pronounce my own nombre—

recordando la chica mala
laughing en la escuela primaria,

mocking me mean girl because
I sound like I am from outer

space when I try to speed through
oraciones as if I am soaring

through the inner spaces
of mi garganta, mi lengua

seems to trip around strangers
extrañas, they glare at me—

their ojos asking, de dónde
eres? I want to speak, hablar

alto, and answer. Even though
sigo vivo, looking like I am

aire muerto choking on palabras
but nada comes out but mi

tartamudear, when everyone
stares at my self-conscious

blushes, feeling like an alien
without a voz, as I try to

converse, when words actually
sneak out, sólo escuchame

between my faltering speechlessness
en español, even gasping to articulate

en inglés, look beyond my tan
piel, all those años I've tried to

enunciate, you will always oír—
my stutter es mi acento.

Seeing Papi Llorando

…for the first time, he
was Mount Everest—

always fearlessly
towering above me

as we sat en la oficina
de la familia terapista

cerca a De Zavala Rd.
San Antonio, 1997,

on that sabado afternoon,
as he sat revealing so much

during his intense therapeutic
interrogation, in the middle

of the room, manos covering
his sobbing, in front

of us, shocked to
see his avalanche

of tears, his lágrimas
almost flooding the room

so quiet, trying to
swim and understand

seeing the Papi who
nunca estuvo triste—

there was the time I saw
him fumando un cigarillo,

mirando Walter Cronkite's
report about la guerra in

Afghanistan circa 1980,
so much worry in all

those puffs of smoke
take me back to our

familia therapy as
él llorró, so loudly

like el estaba llorando
por primera vez, all

those years keeping
it all in, he was our

Old Faithfull, seeing
all those waterworks

gushing out flooding
our ojos, the sight

of witnessing Papi llorar
for the first time,

even Visine couldn't
take away all the rojo

in his eyes, wondering
what happens when

we all make it back
to la casa, seeing him

crying, is it safe to
just be who we used to

be? Are we closer
as a familia or do we

remain en silencio? All
of us back home at

at Summit Crest, our
minds still en la terapia

session processing
Papi llorando so loudly—

as we hide in our own
bedrooms, together alone.

Why Are They Weeping?

From Nick U's 1972 photograph The Terror of War

Even at age seven I always
pondered *Why are the kids*
llorando, running from
the black smoke? While thumbing
through los libros mi Papi stacked
in our home oficina as I questioned:
Why are los soldados lighting
more el huma smoke and ignoring
the babies? More than photographic,
I remember these images speaking
to me through pain flashing: *Where*
are los Papi Y Mami of these niños?
I kept looking trying to find meaning
or any kind of sentimiento through
the eyes of these children: *Why*
are they barefoot on the cold
dead cement? All of these
preguntas I asked as I stared
at this photograph, my father
no tenía respuestas to el miedo
mi Papi felt en mis ojos,
all from mirando *Life* pictures
remembering when I sat next
to the FM stereo speakers,
questions glaring back, holding
'the terror of war' en mis manos
pequeñas, hearing static, no answers
for war as Edwin Star asked on
en radio, *What is it good for?*

Mi Papi mouthed, *absolutamente
Nada*. Pointing to mis oidos,
urging me to listen, *in the end*,
my father me dijo— *es la voz de
la belleza que salvará este mundo*.

I Remember One Saturday Morning When I Was Five...

My Papi took me with him to cash
his paycheck at the bank. As we
walked towards the doors, I asked
him— "*What if I became an Archeologist?*"
This was during the days of *Star Wars*
and the *Lost Ark* of *Raiders* when
everybody wanted to be Han Solo
or Indiana Jones. "*Would you like
it if I became an archeologist?*"
My Papi looked back at me,
he replied— "*It doesn't
matter what I think or want, hijo.
Be what you are.*" Looking back,
I wish I had some paper and my
favorite pluma as I remember all
those times he took me to la pulga
joyfully buying vintage copies of
Mad Magazine, shopping for
rare Ian Fleming James Bond
paperback libros at the West Side Book
Shop as he sipped coffee and I ate
grilled cheese sandwiches at
the Film Flam diner, before
watching *King Kong* at the State
Theatre in Ann Arbor, recordando
estos momentos we shared los juntos,
as he drove me, nunca forcing me
to a certain road, from the passenger
side, as he turned up my favorite

tape from *Who's Next*, although
he was a classical hombre,
humoring his hijo who loved
classic rock, Mi Papi would still turn
it up and sometimes he would have
me steer, his way of encouraging me
to journey in my own direction—
whether it be exploring with an Indiana
Jones fedora or escribiendo poemas
like Neruda, before I even decided, on
our Sabado excursions, no vocational
advice, he wanted me to enjoy the ride.

Cinema Cassian

I took my father ▮▮▮▮▮▮▮▮▮▮▮▮▮▮▮▮▮▮▮▮▮▮▮▮▮▮▮▮▮▮▮,
with his thick Mexican accent, ▮▮▮▮▮
▮▮▮▮ to see a hero ▮▮▮▮▮▮▮▮▮
▮▮▮▮▮▮▮▮▮▮▮▮▮▮▮▮▮▮▮▮▮▮
▮▮▮▮▮▮▮▮▮▮▮▮▮▮
▮▮▮▮▮▮▮▮▮▮▮ onscreen ▮▮▮▮
▮▮▮▮▮▮▮▮▮▮▮▮
▮▮▮▮▮▮▮▮▮▮▮▮▮▮▮
▮▮▮▮▮▮▮▮▮▮▮▮▮
▮▮▮▮Did you notice ▮▮▮▮▮▮▮
▮▮▮▮▮▮▮▮▮▮▮▮▮▮▮
▮▮▮▮▮▮▮▮▮▮▮▮
▮▮▮▮▮▮▮▮▮▮▮▮▮▮▮
▮▮▮▮▮▮▮▮▮▮▮▮
▮▮▮▮▮▮▮▮▮▮▮▮▮▮
▮▮▮▮▮▮▮▮▮▮ Diego Luna
▮▮▮▮▮▮▮▮ his accent ▮▮▮▮
▮▮▮▮▮▮▮▮▮▮▮▮
▮▮▮▮▮ And my dad ▮▮▮▮▮
▮▮▮▮▮▮▮▮▮▮▮▮▮
said▮▮▮▮▮▮▮ so happy▮▮
▮▮▮▮▮▮▮▮▮▮▮▮▮▮ Mexican
actors ▮▮▮▮▮▮▮ in movies ▮▮
▮▮▮▮▮▮ matters.

From **Perl's time&space/
riveralwaysknew** Tumblr post
January 4, 2017

16

Bending With blood— Sangre Me futbol

I can still feel him passing
the legacy golazo—
con mis Papi's ojos
we share the love of
grassy knees celebraciónes,
Univision throated calls,
answering every victory,
wanting, waiting every
bend, kick—especially
when Cristiano scores—
so beautifully— mi vida.
Ask, my wife; yo tengo el
pasión—if soccer's
my religion, match day is
my mass. On grass, she sees
me pray during my 90 minute
whistle sermon, on my own
knees begging triumph me, with one
last cross— ahead, kicking
off my devotion. Listo,
como mi Padre, I am ready
for service to begin.

Mirando Hacia Su Jardin

En her wheelchair
the canvas ready for her
dedos grasping
el cepillo de pintura
but she doesn't want to
color for the sake of colorante,
she wants each red to match
la sangre flowing under her
veins, she wants the verde
to match her zelosa of all
the loud voices, a symphony
of pies y piernas stepping
in soil, she is ready to grow
and squeeze the joys of naranja
all over her canvas but she
cannot feel la amarilla of
the sun— it's all azul,
wishing the sky would
send something more
than blues, nebulas
clouding her palate —
she wants to take a bite
of la morado and chew
the taste that will splatter
the dye that will make
her lona feel more vida—
so she waits for las pinturas
to speak to her, listening
for the dripping to spark
her cuerpo with los colors
staining Frida as she paints
fuming her solitaria.

Recordando Game Six

of the World Series, 1986
as I lay en mi dark cuarto
sobbing, grounded from
TV for poor grades as mi papi
had decreed—& the anger
seeped across my pillow
that night, aún recuerdo
los voces de mis hermanos
y mi papi loudly yelling as
Mookie Wilson's ground ball
rolled, heading towards first
base under Buckner's aging
legs. I never watched
the historic play, duranto
tantos años mis lágrimas
furiosas blurred the ESPN
documentary with my salt.
I only witnessed Los 1986
Mets in replays—now thirty-
five years after that noche,
I am ruminating all mi papi
has done to support and todas
las veces que nos ha ayudado,
so many times, mucho
mas importante than
game-saving moments, in the
end, realizing when I was lost,
felt derrotado and crushed, mi papi
was always there to save el dia.
I know eso importa mas than
Game Six. Still in mis
ojos, despite el pasado, as I hold

the remote, I rewind trying to press
pause on my hurt. For me—1986
will always sting. Some nights I can
still feel mis hermanos joyful screams
defeating me from the other room.

Why Mi Mami Loves You, Rafa Nadal

Mi Mami was nunca just a casual
fan watcher, she was dedicated
following each match in her seat
where she would sit, often drift
off silently drooling in a daze
of dolor y silencio, but when you
Rafa arrived on her TV screen,
placing your Evian and pink
flavored drink diagonally by
your seat on the court, with
every passing shot mi Mami
would reawaken, you siempre
resurrecting her spirit, sometimes
in between commercials, I would
I would often ask her why Rafa?
She would proudly answer
el suda like we sweat, seeing
you race, running down
shots across the court, mi Mami
would tell me, *el juega*
como nosotras trabajamos
seeing you fight for every point
on the court, she would proudly
say, *el persevere like we have*
done, de todos los países who
speak español, from deuce to
cada set and final serve, it was
more than amor, in our casa
there was always love for you,
Rafa. When you would fall
down with exhausted alegría
after Championship point,

like your sweat, after she passed
her spirit always next to me,
I would pour tears remembering
mi Mami's gushing praise for you,
ella me dijo, *cuando gana, todos*
con piel morena ganamos tambien,
with each speech, *Nosotros proud*
of his acento, I now entiendo
her palabras, Rafa, con cada victoria,
tu hablas por todos. When all of us—
watch you, our favorite Spaniard
tennis player, lifting every trophy.
we are all a little victorious. Even hoy
after winning, looking over
at mi Mami's framed foto
as the camera's flashes for you,
the commentator of color
announces how much the crowd
loves focusing on *Nadal's joy,*
I swear I can see from her
photograph, grinning jubilosa
next to me, mirándote on TV,
tengo que decirte Gracias Nadal,
because of tú, wherever she is,
through her smiling sonrisa, Rafa,
mi Mami is always glowing with you.

Smoke Exhaling El Viejo

I have a ghost that smokes
Cubans. I smell them from my
Apartment balcony when
I'm writing. We used
to have a cigar ashtray
in our old casa
that was turtle
carved from Indonesian
wood. The ash
would pile up rounded
like a Tortuga

shell. But sometimes I can
hear him howl *hijo, a cigar*
is just a cigar,
like mi papá would,
his chest-wracking
between each puff,
his coughs grinning
like he was back sun-
burning on the beach,
savoring the body
of his half-smoked Havana.
Just conjuring el olor
reminds me of aromatic
odors of cigars bars
in midtown Manhattan
I would frequent
just to inhale
the presence of El Viejo.
I remember all
of his consejos, *a puff*

of cigar smoke, a spit
of rum to keep
the ancestors happy,
makes you feel like
you're in la tierra
fina. I love turning
on el horno, cocinando
some platos picantes
and setting out dishes
of arroz y frijoles negros
for the ghost. El Viejo's
spirit speaks to me en la
cocina. I can hear him
telling me to add mas
cumin, his salty seasoned
inspiración, urging me to
splash his favorite liquor,
so much steamy smoke
bringing life, fire and
revelation. I try to leave
him some grub because
even though he loves
haunting me, some

nights, I can feel the fuma
rings like puffing thought
clouds. Sometimes when I reignite
words on the page,
I can almost taste fresh
rolled Cubanos
in my apartment.
At those moments, I know
I must have appeased
my father's ghost. I miss
the pool hall smoke
where mi padre would
take me in Miami, exhaling

cigarros, those afternoons
echo, the only times I ever
won with him. No longer
smoking me, no matter
the distance, how I miss
the breaking eight balls
of my father's laughter.

Landscape of Frida Herself

*Cento poem from Mario Monteforte Toledo June 10, 1951
interview, translated by Vivian Arimany, in Frida Kahlo:
The Last Interview*

Universally frustrated creator,
pain is her strength of inspiration,
deeply visceral art of intimacy
for sensual self-body paintings
her eyebrows, emanates, she
memorized her voracious nose,
fearful eyes vaunting thoughts
paint colors isolated fearful
with fascination, Kahlo's
stormy corporeal compositions
commune surrealism oil miracles
accentuate magic tension filled
poetic canvases tangled and
tormented memory,
Frida memorized dreams
strange unraveling faces
like offerings opening the insatiable
curiosity, this muralist appears
when Frida awakens the stars,
saturated fingers press skin crevices,
she loves to squeeze body paintings,
Kahlo's flowerings suggest
a magical imagination,
her flesh speaks to proclaim
Frida, her fervent hands triumph
as life striking portraits of destiny—
God imagines her as the creator.

Watching Mi Papi Chew

Masticando savoring
every bite, seeing
the way he slices

each pancake
with such precision
like a surgeon

making his first incision
but my Papi uses only
this silver utensil, el tenedor,

never his cuchillo,
witnessing how the syrup
oozes like sangre

deliciously bleeding
as my Papi takes
a giant bite. I have never

seen my Papi drip in excess
stains, he is the master
of dining, el maestro

de la comida, after
he clears the plate
my Papi enjoys sitting

back. This is when he becomes
a conductor taking
soft symphonic bites

chewing crescendos
making teeth sounds—
the toothpick his woodwind

strings. cleaning his teeth
with his tongue savoring
until the next meal, like a

general preparing his
next battle. Admiring
how he is el rey of la mesa,

the way mi Papi joyfully
rules every meal, from his
asiento, licking each cuchara,

his boca loves savoring cada
plato, comiendo every last
morsel—always ready for

dessert, seeing him stirring
his favorite after dinner
Cafecito, even before

the bill arrives, my father
is already making mental
reservations, el nunca se

preocupa about the cost.
He never fights it, always
planning the next restaurant

gathering. He lives for
feasting with laughter,
proudly listening to his

barriga, mi Papi loves
feeding the appetite of
his gourmet senses.

What Puro Amor Tastes Like

Our familia during
a Domingo drive,
parado at the stop
light as a middle hijo,
I was always en el
asiento del medio
with my camera like
coke-bottle gafas
seeing everything—
in front manejando
Papi chewing chicle,
leaning over to Mami
for a co-pilot kiss,
as the car horns
honk a symphony of
ruido, mis hermanos
and I en ese momento
instead of being grossed
out niños, we discovered
what puro amor tastes
like… witnessing mi
padre pass the verde
gum from his boca
sweetly inside
my mother's mouth—
with his foot on the break
forgetting about the turn
signal, mirando mi Papi in
love savoring her sabor within
Mami's sweetest beso lips.

One More Stop Till Dairy Queen

Helado was the one thing that
tasted like familia to me.
Those nights after dinner
the five of us walking to
Dairy Queen or other noches
making the even longer stroll
to 'Basket Robins' as mi Mami
called it for sugar coned scoops
of Rocky Road that would melt,
literally drip to the sound of Papi's
laughter on our moon walks
home. Those nights seem so
far away now, Mami keeps telling
us, "We're almost There." Still
two hours from the border
and I could barely swallow,
only tasting the salt in my tears
trying to forget the way mi Mami
left our Papi, separated, ahora esta
soltero in San Antonio. Next
stop Dairy Queen was all I heard
Mami say, but she could see it
from my red ojos, wanting to
go back to those melty cone
nights with Dad. As she passed
the exit, even Mami knew,
I didn't want ice cream, without
Papi, it would never taste the same.

As If He Wanted to Wake Marquez from Beyond his Grave

"The secret of a good old age is simply an honorable pact with solitude."

—*Gabriel Garcia Marquez*

Mi papi disagreed with Gabriel,
for not capturing in *Cien Años*
the whole of soledad.

This was not sacrilegious
in Bogota, since both Papi
and the author are Colombianos,

they drink from the same
passionate botella de licor
of la convicción. But what if

they sipped while contemplating
my theory of soledad outside
of el libro. A celebration of the self!

Isolating oneself from contact
conversations and connections until a state
of mente consciousness is achieved.

Too many cling to each other fearing
solitude because they are terrified
of loneliness.

Solitude has nothing to do
with the drunk despair
of emptiness. Solitude

should be celebrated, for reading
is one of the best cures
for isolationism.

Solitude swims
in a space of tranqualidad.

When I am unaccompanied
I am searching for the love
within myself, if I cannot bear

my own shadow, how
could someone
love me in return?

Mi Papi and Marquez would agree—
nunca estoy solo cuando escribo
mis poemas solitarios.

Mi Mami In My Dreams Again, Anoche

I walked into our old casa
at Burlington Ave. and saw
las señoras de la limpieza
saliendo out of nuestro
garaje as they drove away
I went back adentro and
was immediately hungry
for food. On the counter
en la cocina was cold
McDonalds French Fries.
I called out for mi Mami
but no one was home.
No longer cincuenta años
de edad, inside la casa I felt
like I was fifteen again.
I heard las llaves en la puerta,
as the door opened, mi
Mami was the first one in
the door. She was blushing
excited telling me, Papi
showed her some video
reels of me reading las
poemas de *Sombra*. As she
dropped the grocery bags on
the tiles, Mami told me how
proud she was of the Poems
in *Speaking*. Lo último que
recuerdo is seeing her
standing, Mami beaming
for me, in the doorway—
this is when I woke up
smiling, but I wanted to

go back. My mother left
me desando a longer dream
connection, feeling sombrío
at sunrise for not savoring
this momento together. Quería
volver and leap back into mis
sueños just to hear mi Mami,
but I could not redial. She
remains adentro mi mente
Alegría glowing—far
away and somehow más
cerca inside me.

Sandbox

A memory waves
here, hoy— our AM transistor

crackles "I'm So Young,"
Mami watching

over me in la playa,
with a shovel building

my sandcastle imagination,
the music behind

mis ojos, feeling like
Brian Wilson as

a child, hearing an ocean symphony,
as la agua washes away

my castle, turning around
mi Mami I can no longer

sea her. I can almost hear
her like a canción in the

wind. This Beach Boy
in afternoon low tide,

these hands no longer
digging con miedo, with

mis manos in the sand
rediscovering paradise

in my own isle of view,
stepping outside of my

personal sandbox, I can
stand up solo, all though

she is gone, alone, I am,
no longer trieste.

Con El Mar Behind Me

"I must not fear... I will face my fear. I will permit it to pass over me and through me... Where the fear has gone... Only I will remain."
                                        —*Frank Herbert*

Summer tide rises, la playa
soaks me as I read mi poema a
mi mami, the gulf dissipates

con el sol brilla
intensamente behind me,
ignoring the tidal of fear as

the ocean currents me while
I recite every line, cada stanza,
enunciating every rhyme,

my voice reaching beyond
my blurry glasses as I focus
on floating, the sea esta conmigo,

dedicating every stuttering
syllable, my stammer
emerging brave, like a castle

towering over Newport Beach,
no longer a boychild con miedo,
I am beginning to the glow

adentro, past el capullo of my inner
darkness, feel mi fuerte feet pruning,
butterflying by the second, parado

descalzo— I stand recitando para
mi mami, el mar behind me,
becoming the poem, I am

swallowing mi susto with daylight.

Between My Shadow

*From photograph of Frida Kahlo in Beyond the myth
exhibition at MUDEC of Milan*

I feel most naked
without my canvas
colores, no brushes
no paint on my fingers
no smudges, as el sol
rises, let me hide here
white boda dress see-through
exposing my au natural
color, mi sangre, silencio
avoiding other fiesta voices
toasting chisme, drinking
chistes, tomando laughter
as I glow here in the corner
they want to paint me—
too many whispered drunk
unbottled impressions
they don't want to feel—
oírme, color me over, and
they love to abstract my voice,
I don't belong to Diego,
soy casado, I am wedded
to mis pinturas. They want
to cuadro me, leaving
me displayed to show off
their obra of arte piece,
hanging in oscura darkness,
I am more than a painting
standing here between

mi sombra invisible,
sin beauty mascara
no concealer, on my face—
I am a masterpiece unfinished.

For My Lover, Returning to Her Husband

I closed my mouth and spoke to you in a hundred
silent ways.

                                    —*Rumi*

Some nights, I wish I was still
there, the way she looked at me

ringing the bell, licking her
lips, I was her favorite room

service dish, her husband
was mild, she had a taste

for picante, extra flavor. "Speak
to me, in Spanish" she demands,

always in control, she sees me
sizzling ready to eat. I can tell

the way she bites into me,
I have a spicy aftertaste,

devouring me like guacamole.
But she is not hungry for an

appetizer, her eyes look at me
like I am carne asada. With each

bite, she fills up with her
carnal appetite. So selfish

each drop that she steals,
drinking me up like shots

of tequila. I just want to be
more than the limón in her

mouth. The same one she
spits out. Until she desires,

dessert, am I just a postre
with extra creama whipped?

She will never let me be
on top like a cherry. I remain

the caramello stain on the side
of her smeared lipstick mouth.

Pushing me off her, I wish
she would leave a hint of me,

there, a sticky reminder
of her medianoche craving

from our time together, but
before she returns to her

husband, she uses her tongue
and makes me disappear by licking

me off. No longer tempted
by her hunger, she leaves

me like a dirty afterthought—
feeling so unsatisfied.

The Secret Muse of Gabriel Garcia Márquez

"Just as a snake sheds its skin, we must shed our past over and over again."

—*Buddha*

He saw her at el aeropuerto
in Paris, waiting to board
in line para el avión to JFK,
Nueva York en la terminal
internacional at Charles
de Gaulle. While he was
scribbling down an idea
on his boarding pass, el no
se dio cuenta the next chapter
of his life stood en frente
de este escritor. When her
perfumed scent arrived
landing in his airspace
the author dropped his pen,
él nunca olió nada tan deslumbrante
como su esenciahe from this
most captivating passenger.
He tried to come up with
the most magically realistic
lines to describe her essence
but he just stood there asombrado,
in complete awe of the way her
long hair, perfectly combed
flowed in front of him like
dark Basin of São Francisco—
sending secret waves, he wanted
to speak but her tight blanca
summer dress distracted him,

as she held up her Brazilian
passport, the writer glimpsed
her nombre, Silvana de Faria.
In his mind, Gabriel Garcia
kept pronunciando her name,
over and over. He heard
the airline attendant scanning
boarding passes, as the line
moved, he wanted to speak
to her, to enunciate Silvana's
name like Neruda would when
reciting una love poem to one
of his paramours. He kept
saying her name, Silvana,
over and over mouthing it
as if he was preparing to read
a line from one of his most
famous libros. But before
Márquez could speak up,
his courage failed him.
Silvana realized she was
at the wrong gate, she
picked up her carry on
luggage, and with her
giant purse hanging
from her softest slender
brazos, she sauntered
away, her high heels
clicking, resounding
the most beautiful echo,
the same cumbia like
percussion that would
haunt his sueños for years.
Replaying this moment in
his mente, una y otra vez,
wishing he could rewrite a
final feliz when they would

run off together to a hotel
by the airport, leave the
do not disturb on la puerta,
never checking out—
reawakening his secret muse,
between Gabriel Garcia's
unwritten sheets, leaving this
famoso autor Colombiano
pondering a vida of a hundred
more years of solitude.

We Finally Learned Heaven is Avocado

I slow glide into the circle,
fold myself into the night,

smell your body, the scent
of the mole, above

your piloncillo palms, memory
to recreate you, amber moon,

golden skin, this face a lantern,
singing *muy enamorado*,

remember you, the boy I kissed,
I miss the dark, hands

that pleasure inside, bodies
so close, I love completely,

next to your back, awake
the scent of jasmine milk

circling above your *Papacito*
weightlessness, every crevice

tender tortillas, your elegant
filthy fingers, speak tender

moist eyes frothy wider opening,
I fluttered my sticky vanilla

oozed honey, beneath joy
arrived, you came trembling

your hungry mouth delirious
to eat the murmur magic,

my animal language
mi Purísima corazon

ojos hollering, *Ay*,
my belly pleasure sweetened

us tangled between syllables
that whispered our swirling

love, your tongue gently
sucked, yes, pressed between

kisses, my legs felt the mango
joy of our fruit navel mornings.

Cento Poem from "Eyes of Zapata" in Sandra Cisneros' Woman
Hollering Creek

Simple ■ Complicated

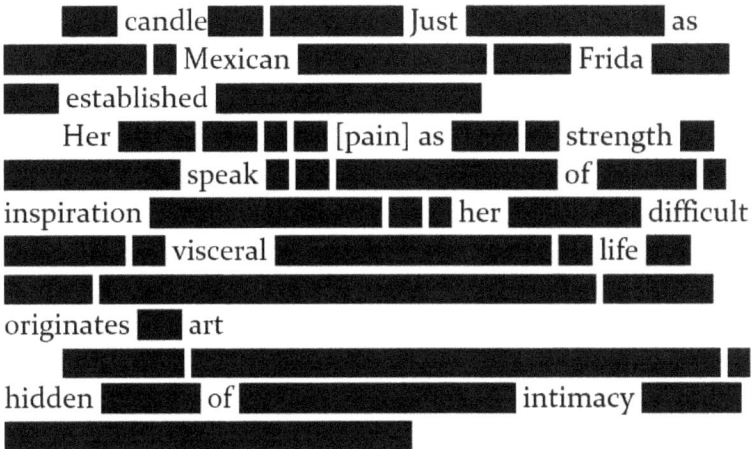

████ candle███ ████████ Just ██████████████ as
████████ ■ Mexican ████████████ ███ Frida ████
███ established ███████████████
Her ████ ███ ■ [pain] as ████ ■ strength ██
████████████ speak ■ ■ ███████████ of ██████ ■
inspiration █████████████ ██ ■ her ███████ difficult
████████ ■ visceral ████████████ ■ life ██
████ ███████████████████████ ████
originates ███ art
████████ ██████████████████████ ██
hidden ██████ of █████████████ intimacy ████
████████████████████

From "Frida Landscape of Herself"
interview by Mario Monteforte Toledo
Novedades: Mexico en la Culture
June 10, 1951
Translated by Vivian Arimany

II:

"You can't erase what you know.
You can't forget who you are."

— **Sandra Cisneros**

I Once Saw Frida Kahlo

I heard the Lady under
the old Mexican mausoleum
in tune with the purest
marble, Deco meringue
interior, sweeping tastes
of glass decorated of
Rivera, the art culminating
in a sanctuary of pantheon
lights those sumptuous murals
of magnificent woman
volcanoes of Mexico. Kahlo
entered jangling metallic
jewelry, in concert look,
discover her rhythms beyond
the orchestra sounds, physical
the noise mother of serpents,
bloody brooch lacerated Aztec
vulture rooted herself deity of
pectorals transforming claws
like Cleopatra, herself, depicting
a spectacular century woman—
her infinite body corsets
shriveled broken protected
the cartwheels dusk of moon
devouring light showing
Kahlo supreme fine
smoking upwards, her
wings announced a magnetism,
like the throb exhibiting Frida
as the butterfly, Goddess.

*Cento poem from Carlos Fuentes Introduction in The Diaries of
Frida Kahlo*

No Toques el Cristal

Mami would mouth, her
lips moving loudly,
slapping her hands
gesturing how she would

castigar all of us, even
when she whispered
in our large house it felt
like she was gritando,

telling us not to touch
her glass figurines. It
always seemed like
part of our casa, Mami's

half was like a museo,
where we couldn't touch
anything. Mami
was already the security—

guarding her precious
breakables. All we needed
was a velvet rope like the
ones they have at el banco.

I always wonder what she saw
in these glasspieces? We called
them the untouchables. The same
ones she would gently speak,

to each one, as if they were
the plants outside. When she

54

was napping, I would sit
and watch how Mami's

glass figurines would glow
en el sol in the afternoon
radiating rainbows, Even
la senora who would come

clean our casa was very
cuidado while dusting
feathers around these
collectibles. One time
she accidently knocked
over one of the porcelains
kissing couple that Papi
had gifted our mother

for their aniversario.
I watched Mami
superglue the neck
of the boy who was

temporarily beheaded.
After the glue dried,
I would often sneak up
and look at his neck,

waiting for el sol to shine
her arco iris to magically
bring him back to life
so he could kiss the amor

of his life one last time.
I would imagine him
leaning in tasting her
lips, even at that age

I could tell they were
a well chiseled work
of art. Even I wanted
to kiss her. I bet they

never knew how much
Mami cherished and
loved each one of these
figurines. Now these glass

pieces are wrapped in storage,
boxed near the ark of the covenant.
I bet even in darkness, los cristal
wait for the sun to glow the spirit

of my mother—I wish I could
tell each one of her immortally
intocables she truly misses all
of her fragile friends.

If Heaven had waiting horas...

With my feet in the clouds
I would sit esperando for
you behind the door of la luz—

Hearing angels wings flapping
beautifully, leading all of those with
visitors to the clear waiting room

in the sky, as each familia, esposa,
husband, niña, brother, hermana,
entering on el otro lado de la puerta—

we could overhear the joyful
abrazos, tears and such powerful
light coming from the other

side. Restlessly waiting, I can
already hear you telling me
paciencia hijo mio, and then

mi nombre called in between
harps, as I rise, the door opens
and there you are glowing

ageless sonrisas. Reaching
you, Mami, feeling your magical
manos touching my cheek,

telling me how much you love
mi corto haircut, y abrazamos
until I feel a tap on the shoulder,

whispering to let me know
time's up, but I do not want
to let go, eyes closed and

then all I feel is clouds, you
disappear, inside me, otra
vez. I wake up en mi cama

tears on my pillow, already
for the next time I am able
to sit in the cielo room

embracing this moment mágica,
and waiting to spend a heavenly
minute, abrazarte eternally.

Gracias Faby Ryan

When my Little Hermano Talks
to the Spirit of our Mami

[in the middle of his Amazon Warehouse job in San Antonio, TX]

No next day, just
like Prime she arrives
in less than an hour
when he feels the weight,
so much my brother,
carries for his five bella
niñas and his own beautifully
preciosa wife, en la casa,
sometimes, he tries to hide,
when the tears arrive, his llorando
feeling too heavy, this
is when her voz appears
to sooth his dolor. Even
after so many años
the empty space inside
rivals the warehouse work,
filled with so many unopened
boxes of emotions, he keeps
locked adentro. He keeps
trying to crack the seal as
our Mami's voice whispers...
*Hijo, take it easy, I know
esta es mucho para ti. Keep
moving derrecho.* Mi hermano
adjusts his hearing aids
when the speaker announces
another shipment, he loves
when she answers, past

the cielo rafters, hablando
palabras, my brother heeds her
wisdom inside his head,
resounding the signals
of his hearing aids—
she's far
from dead at work, in
the middle of the Amazon
warehouse, he stops, waiting —
claramente, siempre she appears.

Lucky Trece, Septiembre 13

On so many other days
I had failed so many
times. Recuerdas el dia

cuando you wouldn't even
let me manejar to the Texas
DMV to take my driver's exam.

We all lost count of the no pass,
so many FAIL stamps on my
driver's permit, would I ever

be able to take the wheel solo?
So many tests, so many more
times, driving home feeling

more than wrecked. I could
hear you already, *Nuca*
lo permit a manejar on

my own. My one front seat
flaw, unable to park parallel,
the floppy cones, my enemigos,

y una vez speeding through stop
signs. Another time I took
the exam with a Texas DPS

trooper in the front seat tobacco
chewing, all grins intimidating
me with his mirror shades and

when he would spit into his paper
cup, my nervous soles, ready to
accelerate, instead of drive, putting

the car in reverse, scaring the officer
who jolted in the passenger seat—
otra vez, test over, another FAIL

stamp. So many more times, leaving
the DMV dejected wondering would
I ever earn my license?

And then el día arrived...
a gift, a reprieve on your cumpleaños—
this time Mami, I could feel you, so

close, yet far away, above my rearview
mirror cheering me on as I perfectly
parallel parked and as I drove back

from the DMV on Babcock Ave,
the volunteer tester handed me
el papel con las noticias buenas—

finalmente, on your birthday,
lucky 13th, always because of
you, like now, so many años

later, you appear so much
closer. I feel you above, looking
apendiente, cuando manejo,

escribo mis poemas, now always
there, even when I cannot see
you, spotlight me when I am on stage,

you are la luz of belief that appears
siempre closest always cerca conmigo.

Flores Para Los Muertos

Hearing the glimmers between
every footstep walking con
la memoria de mi abuelito, lo
sentirlo holding my quivering
manos en el cementerio. Feeling
los espíritos, santos vivendo in
el viento, seeing each grave etched
in R.I.P., although I am surrounded
by triesteza stone as I stand
among the llorando espíritu
welcoming the wind—shivering
mi piel ignites goose-bumping
skin within us all these spirits—
I listen to las voces, blowing
whispers through the leaves,
no longer con miedo among
the tearful signing crosses,
beyond the suits y vestidos
regalos de silencio and prayers,
finger besos for los living
muertos, siempre still flowing,
closing mis ojos— embracing
these whispers intensely welcoming
pensamientos awakening sonrisas
of eternity, in my head I am
no longer haunted. Mis ojos
now open por la primera vez,
forgetting the darkness, smelling
more than los flores—
with my mind abierto to

this beautiful presence—
feeling so many familia spirits
blinking light through me.

Starry, Starry Light

"Every star may be a sun to someone."
            —*Carl Sagan*

Every time you would take
us to el mueso when mis
hermanos and I would run

off, muchas horas despues
we would find you with
su Walkman headphones in

your ears, escuchando
your favorite Don McLean
canción, on repeat, standing

in front of the one piece
you would gaze, mirandolo
contemplating the palates

parado frente a la obra de
arte, in love con la noche
en el lienzo, the peaks

curling above el pueblo,
imaginando todos en la
cuidad dormiendo while

sus ojos focus amazed
at the glowing estrellas
amarillas beaming circulos,

so many waves of azules
swimming en el cielo sky.
I wish haberte preguntado

what made this Van Gogh
piece su pintura favorita.
I imagine the colors like

Vincent's brushstrokes
would instantly reflect
like olas in the sky and

ripple your secreto sadness
in waves. Instead of kneeling
in church, the museum became

one of your most devoted
sacred espacios. Sus ojos
no longer watching Dios,

the only hymn you live
to oir, concentrating on
this starry night, with your

eyes gleaming, los colores
would sing to you— no
longer triste listening

always picturing paradise,
focusing on your favorite masterpiece
seeing you, Don McLean

in your ears siempre serenading
you, Mami's eyes resounding
with the brightest of blues

glimmering vida colors of delight.

I Love Him Madly

I can see him sitting
there, book in his lap

always wearing a mask,
mi padre a superhero—

even con gafas
fearless ojos,

above his mascara,
setenta años viejo

and eternally fuerte
strong— mi Papi,

I always read him
as ageless, on this

flight, he is like
a Miles Davis trumpet

that sits there, floating
en el éter and then

the presence of memory,
the melody of each note

of his voz, his sonrisa
the laughter echoing

like a wah wah trumpet
of *Get Up With It—*

is what he would
tell me, advice that

would always soar
over my immature

cabeza, like hearing
Calypso Frelimo,

but mi Papi
como Davis had

a fusion like
way to reach

his wandering
hijo. Lost in stanzas

finding myself on
poems waiting to

be crafted.
"Encuentra tu propio

camino," Papi
would tell me,

knowing I was
living my life

like a Quintet
improvisation,

nómada exploring
el mundo, just

like he is again
as I write this

flying down to
Colombia—

at times I seemed
in a hurry, going

nowhere rapido.
Papi was always

patient, sometimes
furioso but he always

believed in me even
when we weren't

hablando. Despite
la distancia of our

silencio, siempre
pendiente conmigo

especially after
Mami passed,

Papi was more
than a telefono

call away, "lo que
nececitas," he would say,

sometimes it was
simply a weekly

conversación
between padre

e hijo. Some
semanas we would

read the same libro
and talk about

the chapters we loved.
other days, we shared

our favorite plays
from the soccer

matches, texting
did you see that

golazo? An escritor
like me, we talked

books, articles,
arte, política del

amor y la vida.
He was nervioso

telling me about
his first novia

after Mami,
I listened and

was excited for
Him. I already

want to call him,
seven plus dias

is a long time,
mas tiempo

than a cut from
Get Up With It,

so many Miles
and I wait,

trying not to
let mi mente

spin in worry,
I listen to side

two: "It's
About Time"

hope he lands
soon, I am

eager for our
diálogo to continue,

two minds and voices
we musically groove—

siempre connecting
In a Silent Way.

Ella era la Silenciosa

Mi Abuelita Zoila rarely
spoke to us when she
arrived en el avion

desde Bogota. She would
nod and sit next to mi
abuelito who was even

quieter than my abuela
who would always instruct
my abuelito to hush. She

always spoke for him, even
when they visited my room,
although we didn't hablar

the same lengua, yo naci
Americano y sentí her
frialdad cuando mi abuelita

Colombiana talked down
to me in Spanish. Para unir
el lenguaje gap, I would spin

canciones from Los Beatles
White Album. She would sit
on a chair cerca de mi and nod

her cabeza to the universal rhythms
of "Ob-La-D- Ob-La-Da."
As I would turn over each side

of los discos, with each song,
I noticed her thaw, she was
not the frozen reina I was

warned about ella era la
Silenciosa. Rarely smiling
I felt a change while we sat

in my room, barely hablando,
as I sang along to Paul cantando,
Sing it loud so I can hear you—

For the first time, I saw her grinning
as I sang, *Make it easy to be near*
you, although we could not speak,
at that time, I only stuttered en

ingles, seeing her smile, while we
connected to el disco spinning
en mi cuarto, nunca olvidaré

ese día, exchanging giggles—
we no longer familia extraños
when our ojos y orejas unimos

joyously, la unica tiempo we
understood each other con la
música speaking for nosotros

con la lengua de los Beatles.

Ode to Don Jose

Our Colombian citizen, wooden
caned, mi abuelito walking gigantic
larger than life like his stories

his legend massively enlightening,
always sprinkled so refined—
Imagining a hero, my grandpa

and his belly so boisterous like Brando—
he was so suave in his grey suits,
white camisas like his chauffeured stories,

so many he would share with me, taller tales,
white winks and his cerveza like beard
dipped in whiskey whistles, dazzling drunk

chatter topped off with the coolest flicks
of his smokiest Marlboro laughter.
When I blink back to his barrio drives

showing me the diablo's nose on mountain peaks
swerved me dizzy, with that secret scent I was
not allowed to cultivate with sight nor accent.

At dusk as mañana crooned, so did mi abuelo
cantando in his lengua romantica, echoing
around his casa, always the first awake,

baño steaming as his kitchen whispers
calmly stirring his sueños. Mi abuelo eagerly
awaited the delivery of his eyed wide leche—

arrived daily pouched in Colombian plastico,
he always allowed me to cut the milk,
watching me pour the whitest sensation

inside, summoning the steam like spirit
of his simmering bowl— I recall staring at the horno
rising when boiling, remembering his chowder,

sweetest Bogota tasting, his favorite cilantro
recipe dishes, recalling his taste buds
as my grandfather flavored fun. Extra-large

chef finger rhythms, beaming stew while
dancing Colombian cumbias en la cocina
always sharing his stories while chewing

as his cuchara bent through clouds of
laughter— I learned hints of his fearlessness
from watching his voz. Like a legend,

more than a god, I favored every
momento he led— my personal Simón
Bolívar, so statuesque my grandfather

Don Jose, I still make the cross while pouring
his holy water with some drips of brew
on concrete in his honor— there's no other

way to share him, his laughter lived so jovial—
mi abuelito, my giant, his legacy the most
interesting hombre, his shadow was sweet—

still picturing him so harmonious, Don Jose
always surrounds me, standing large
with his cane, even taller cementing

his voz, flickering lighters in his honor,
when puffing Marlboro Red's, I exhale
my smoke skyward towards

his cloudy eyes, as his lighter grins
and matches the cantos, so sweet,
in my head, hearing him sing—

he still ignites fires—
mi abuelito's advice
I always will repeat.

Mi Abuelito told us Hombres Never Wear Medias to Bed

Este viejo would tell us these
cuentos while taking off his
own socks before bed, one
of the many consejos he would
share with us, because we were barely
adolescents, no pelo on our chest, so young
without sin or músculos, mis hermanitos
and I would immediately ignore him. We
were all Mama's boys, with little
or any toughness or tenacidad. Can
you tell that our abuelito came from
the school of old? Mirando hacia atrás,
este viejo and his machismo ways would
be so outdated in our dias modernos.
A grey-haired relic con his Diego Rivera
barrriga, with a cerveza thirst for laughter,
his art was being a narrador of tales
exagerados. The bigger the story,
nosotros creímos, believing his tales
like the devil's nose from the side
of la montaña on the winding calle
to Bogota was actually chiseled by
el diablo himself. Despite the lack
of la verdad, ahora que tengo canas
of my own, I now sleep, under our covers,
without socks. Although I will never
be the kind of hombre he wanted mis
hermanos and I to become— recuerdo
how wrong este viejo was but as I try

to drift off into sueños, me doy cuenta
that it took me cincuenta años and I still
escuché to his cuentos even though
I shiver bajo these frio bedsheets.

Does an Hombre Have to Die to Speak to His Own Father?

Papi, I don't want to wait to
tell you, por favor, please—
trim those eyelashes and

your ear hairs, they have been
way too long for muchos años that's
how long I remember us being

estranged. I used to tell mis amigos
we only spoke every cuatro años,
during la Copa Mundial, and los

elecciones presidential. I used to
believe we were so diferente, you
always towering above, overshadowing

me. Now I realize you were mi guía
to protect me, not ground me. I know,
lo sé, you helped me harness my voice

I found in la poesía. Whenever I had
any doubts, you always encouraged me
to *sigue tu propio camino*, my own path

I followed, even when I asked, who am I?
An author? Published? Me dijo, *own this,
hijo*. I listened, *te oí*, I did and now con

every libro, book, volume, chapbook, review,
you always gush Papi proud. I don't want to
wait to tell you, I am a poet because of you,

Soy Poeta! No longer eclipsando, even millones
of miles away you are always at the side of
my stage. Seeing the spotlight glowing on

my presencia, did you know, you gave me
the entusiasmo gift of mis palabras? I learned
to savor the art of reading from you. I also,

don't want to wait to decirte, you have
the best laugh, I miss the bolstering sound
of joy radiating around the room, when your

cheeks are puffy rojo, riendo red. En serio,
Gracias por el regalo de mis palabras. And
every time I stutter behind the podium,

microphone I become, su hijo, the sun, yo
soy Ernesto, recitando I have the strength
to stand, pararse derecho— soy agradecido,

abrazos, Papi, I more than listened—orejas
abiertos—su hijo siempre, lo escuché.

Gracias Juan Gabriel Vasquez

Hello, Mi Viejo Amigo

"Slowdown/slow… down"
  — *Thomas Edward Yorke*

Somedays I feel like
un turista in my body,
a stranger perdido con
garngata coughing
in my chair, like
las estrallas in the
noche sky, I could
count every memory—
my internal tree ring's
each wrinkle skin
remembering her labios
melting me with the first sparks
of winter snow kisses and
I can still taste her
besos, our shivering
smiles are markers, tattoo
recuerdos that make each
segundo a momento of
resilience as time signals us—
each ache resounds
the ticking of the internal
clock like our abuelos, we are
becoming hourglass tourists,
so many bags packed under
our eyelids, reflecting how
many pulsations are left…
Do we countdown la horas?
Daydreaming a dance to los
ritmos by letting everyone

know, we hold our beats
from within and cada día
we amanecer ojos closed,
bailando, we glide—
adentro, no matter how old
giggling on this sofa—
we remain almost unbeaten.

between each fall

In invierno mornings,
I try to embrace myself. I want
to lift open my sockets
and stop evading my gaze
between the moody
ojos shadowing, spring,
verano, glaring back
at me, whatever cara,
pimpled warts, and all—
glancing again at this imperfect
pánico, trying as i struggle
con todo hambre to stare,
trato de abrazarme, I hunger
to be proud and glare, instead
all atención at the mouth, labios
chapped for too long i have been
silent with dolor. i am tired of
picturing myself mirando down,
away at the vidrio. i leave the luz
off, i try not to tip toe into
el baño. instead of eyes,
all i see are the excess piel
and bags in the spaces donde
llevo all the weight of my
revolving second thoughts. i fear
los pensamientos as my reflections
constant catcalls shattering me
deeper adentro, these black holes
debajo my eyelids, por qué no
puedo mirar mi extraño face?
Quien es este sleepless stranger
disperto, mirándome en el espejo?

I brace the sink as the glass
cackles with cutting respuestas
que nunca quiero sentir.

Ode to her Unibrow

"You did not understand what I am. I am love. I am pleasure, I am essence, I am tenacious. I am; simply I am..."

—F.K.

They couldn't see why
every wrinkling arrugado
dimple, every cicatriz scar
bellowing above
your curepo's prickliest
equator, the short hair,
pelo uncurled the way you
downed half-full botellas
of vinos, shots of tequilas,
perfumed boquillas exhaling
fuma smoke from the side
of your labios, the aftertaste
smoky so hermosa from the longing
of your after-midnight beso kisses.
Every inch reflected a canvas,
each painful refrain, each
awkward sonrisa smile
reflecting a part of your nombre.
Art is not something that comes
from los dedos, each gripping
view of your paintings—
cada uno oozes with aches
that shakes from your manos,
demanding more
than a life, your vida
reflecting a face hauntedly
encantado with grace, colorful

brushes combing all your pleasures—
evoking todo fracturado,
the broken trying to reveal
the essence of your agony—
framing a corazon consumed
with exposing a single
entrancing piece, a part
of the unibrow vision—
that is Frida Kahlo.

La Señora de La Jolla, CA

Inside the caves, I envision
the silhouette of Frida Kahlo
stoically standing above
the waves, her outline
beautifully viviendo in this spirit,
she no longer needs a brush,
the ocean is her canvas as her
profile loves to paint the shape
of tides, surfs, and the colors
of the costal blues, sunset
skyline of yellow, orange
and hints of greens. Past
the rocks, I envision you,
Kahlo smoothly outlining
colors. Los sueños silently
greets you con the spirit
of las olas. The sea drenches
as you love immersing in
el mar of your dreams.
When you stand
reawakening la Señora
of La Jolla, awestruck over
looking across las cuevas
of your seabed view,
Frida's silueta, pintando
the horizon splashing
your senses as la oceánica
soaks through.

We share the same threshold of dolor

El agonía I feel when
I am curled on the tiles
next to the toilet, en el
baño, I remember the pain
when you Mami were in el
hospital for food poisoning,
whenever I am enfermo
from digestive dolor, I realize
nosotros tenemos the same
delicate stomach. Our only
choice of foods to eat is bland.
Anything too salty or spicy
causes eruptions through our
gargantas from la bariga. I now
know why you ate cream of
wheat for desayuno y sopa
for dinner, it was all your estómago
could handle and I am the same
like you, always nibbling on
very blanda dishes, and when
el dolor returns en la mañana
siguiente, after fighting another
early morning bout of food
poisoning, I am always playing
comeda detective trying to
figure out what I ate that made me
so sick. Although, I recall all
the laughter we giggled los
juntos, it's when I am suffering
for eating the wrong foods,
sick todo el día, me doy cuenta
of the pain we share swallows

us both— when I am in agony
in the bathroom, I feel closer
to you, su hijo—lo mismo,
ambos nos duele—the same.

I Dreamt We Spoke Again

I remember en mis sueños
when I answered you
once again desde el otro
lado, although you were
so far, just to hear su voz
resounding so much closer
from the other side, recuerdo
preguntándote, *where are you*?
There was a pause as I held
escuchandote on speaker,
I wanted everyone in this
room to hear you Mami,
that although you had passed
I was talking to you, pressing
record, wanting mi Papi y
mis hermanos to oír me
hablando contigo. As I asked
How are you? as if you were
on a viaje. I remember
you answered, *Estoy bien,
hijo*. Even in my dream, you
no querías que me preocupara.
In between la estática y
silencio, I wanted to stay talking
to you forever. Recuerdo, feeling
you smile on the speaker side
of mi telefono. As I replayed
my phone call to Papi,
all he could hear
was his son hablando con static.

In my dreams when we talked
so close, en mis sueños speaking
to me, sintiendo your voice—
resonante hearing you, muy
cerca clear.

I was on my knees

"The floor seemed wonderfully solid. It was comforting to know I had fallen and could fall no farther."
—Sylvia Plath, *The Bell Jar*

Under eyes filled with
so much baggage,
feeling jetlagged
without leaving
our two-bedroom LA
apartment. Sleepless
for so many días,
my mind confused
much more than dazed
could not remember
what day it was. When
I finally asked for ayuda,
the help I had been
fearing to preguntar for too
many años, this darkness
de depresión had over-
shadowed me, for
so long, I felt the trail
of this disorder phantom
had become part of me—
part of the boy who
was splashing tears
of grief for his Mami
that had passed away
three years before and
I still had not want to
face the gaping depths of
the hueco she left in

mi vida. On that day,
en el piso, sabiendo
que no podía caer
más, gripping my cell,
con miedo en mis rodillas
llamando mi papi, knowing
I needed away to swim
out of this hole I created
with my fears that tidal me
terrified. And from the other
side of el telefono, calling
for help, for the first time,
no more shame. I felt splashes
of hope as the grip of his mano
began to slowly lift me, his
consejos showing me
the ways to swim myself
out from my darkness
to the luz. I was drenched
in desperation, soaked in
sadness, slowly ascending
from the bottom finally,
reaching up
for my father's distant
dial tone, enunciating
the first words of
por favor, ayúdame, I was
finalmente ready to help
illuminate me from the inside.

She Lives For Sangre

The blood that she has
witnessed oozing outside
every scabbing wound
since the first time she
was impaled in the back
of an autobus, as the metal
pilar thrust inside her
abdomen, besides el dolor
she remembers el sangre
gushing out like the tomatoes
she would squash in her hands
but this had a different flavor,
staining the seats with blood,
her white school summer dress
and on the skin, this color she
could never wash off. When Frida
painted she chose the dye that
matched the spurting out, sticking
to her fingers, dropping the brush
wishing la pintura tasted like
el sangre that once flashed
la muerte but now has given
her more than life, a vida
of sangre she loves painting
veins swelling self-portraits
mirroring the memory that
gave her the masterpiece marrow
that eternally drips the flushed
crimson plasma, her opus
magnum lona revealing—
Frida's canvas bleeding anew.

The language

██ antepasados ████████████ connects ██ our
████████████████ life ██ Some ██ have ██
lost █████████████ ████ Sometimes █████
█████████ harmed █████████████ for
speaking ██ native ██████████████ **save** ████
███████████████████████ ██
███████████ our culture ███████ forever ████████
████ with █████ our ***corazon***.

From **Sandra Cisneros'**

A House of My Own: Stories from My Life

(Vintage International) 2015

III:

*"I've said before that the most important words,
for me, in poems are the words that aren't written,
las palabras that say, 'Yo también.'"*

— **Ada Limón**

Mi Cuerpo

They teased me
on the playground,
always calling me—
El Flaco. I was so bony,
often ignored because
of my lack of lbs,
I was always wanting
a girl to notice me in
the hallway at school.
I hated looking at
myself en el espejo,
always ignored,
not just another traditional
case of middle child
disease, thinking
of myself as the invisible
almost-man. Hombre,
me encantaba a ver
The Incredible Hulk
series, my idealized
reflejndo and seeing
myself a David Banner,
estabe cansado de being
bullied and picked
on for being so skinny,
siempre desando to
TV channel mi furia,
wishing I could turn
into The Hulk.
It never happened.

My Boss Called Me Taco

He only saw the picante
of my skin, imagined I sweat
dolor with a cilantro flavor,
con sal y limón, I wonder
if he thought mi Papi was
a burrito and mi Mami
a spicy quesadilla, mis
hermanos were churros
and we only drank Coronas
or Tecacte instead of sipping jugo
de naranja for desayuno, and
after dinner we down shots
of Tequila. My boss thought
he was being comical, promises
it's all a belly chuckle, only
seeing me as food, I am more
than comida—mi furia
is picante, my sangre does
not bleed salsa. Before he fired
me, giggling, that he was ready
to toss me on the grill, where I
belonged, I wanted to show
my boss he only lived to mix
it up, he could never take
a verbal fruit punch. I know
he was jealously celoso, a tasteless
simple salchicha link no one
wanted to nibble and how mis
novias craved the sizzled tan
of mi carne asada cuerpo skin.
He always stood there smelling
cochino like rotten leche knowing

that she loves to savor me like a
tall glass of horchata and when
he goes home, no longer superior,
always overshadowed, la esposa
his own boss, he lazy
boys, wishing he could
taste like taco, knowing
he's only whipped cream.

Gracias Myriam Gurba

Del Taco is not Poetic

Poetry is sizzling your own
fresca tacos in a pan,
chopping pollo, spinach,
adding queso and corn,
tomates, cilantro, pimientos
de todos colores, like she
taught me cada Tuesday,
and now, in her memoria,
I love stirring mis sentidos
while frying, mi nariz
always inhaling estas aromas
picantes — Por qué drive thru
Taco Bell and eat processed
cochinada when you can
create a feast for your senses.
Cocinando es mi poesia, cada
plato my stanza, rhyming each
dish con sal, pimento,
seasoning each dish is
a poem ready to be
devoured. Each taco calling —
"Cómeme"
seductively boca-watering.
Each bite announces
the satisfied sounds of
my unquenchable hambre.
Savoring cada sabor, even
my paramour knows—
la cocina is my favorite
part of our casa, donde me
encanta crafting culinary
creations in our apartamento—
flavor is home.

Siempre the one afuera del círculo

Watching everyone
in the circle running
around jugando y riendo
and I siempre soy la única
always la solitaria
in the shadow, no one
else wanted to play
conmigo. I was nunca ever
chosen to play with any equipo,
left out in any grupo, who
would want to divertirse con
la flaca? I was the one always
feeling enferma, with my teddy
bears watching from mi cuarto,
invisible from todos las vecinas—
I had no friends, solo compañeras
de clase who ignored me en
la escuela as I ate mi almuerzo
sola. Yo era la extraña, even
in high school, we moved so
much that they called me
the strange nueva loner—
I felt invisible as others
gathered, giggling
chismando at tables full
as I was left nibbling alone
con mi sanduiche de peanut
butter and jelly, sipping
Capri Sun in the shadows—
would I always feel like
the child watching desde
afuera? All I wanted was

to be the one tanning smiles
gathering with the others
en el sol. Sick in my bedroom,
I would dream of being the one
finally building castles
in the sand, sonriendo inside
the circle con una compañera,
who would one day pick up
su teléfono, and call me—
their friend.

Waiting at the Gate, for Mi Novia, Sept 1998, San Antonio International Airport

This had been the first time
we had been away from each
other. This was before texts,
instant messaging, even emails—
we just had letters, post cards,
rarely sending words, dial-up
and telephones were the only ways
we could intimately communicate
with our voices. I waited, wanting to
feel mi novia, the way she always
tastes of Irish coffee in the morning,
at the gate, waiting for her with flowers,
rosas, her favorite, as I kept seeing
so many strangers, her co-workers
she never introduced me to, wondering
if they know about me? What she
says about the flaco novio who
writes her poesias, letras, filthy
love notes, remembering she brought
everything I wrote her, like the time
we had our first getaway to New
Orleans, she said, *if we don't make
it make it, quiero morirme
with your palabras en mis brazos.*
My words in her arms, this how
much I know ella me ama, she
loves me. Waiting to see mi amor,
this is when I spot her, I excitedly
wave, holding up the bouquet of
flowers as she slowly walks my way,

with her bellbottom pants that make the sultriest
swishing noises as she strolls across
the airport. I run up to Ana as I kiss
her but he labios seem distant. She
doesn't seem feliz to see me. I hand
her the rosas and she seems more
annoyed than grateful. *I got you this,*
she says, handing me this long, huge
number two pencil. Standing there at
the airport, I feel not worthy of pen,
I was filled with Lloyd Dobler envy.
She gave me a pencil, it felt like I could
tell from her rolling eyes—she already
wanted to erase me, instead.

A Donde Esta mi Mama y Papa?

"You've got to tell me, brave captain, why are the wicked so strong? How do the angels get to sleep when the devil leaves his porchlight on?"

— *Tom Waits*

I picture ICE soldiers
mocking all the crying
niños y niñas waiting
for their moms and dads
to come home, but you
had them picked up,
rounded up, herded like
animals in the land of Dixie.
Only cater to those Confederate
states with no mind who
burn crosses, now they
love burning effigies
by weaponizing my race,
the aim...anyone who has
a tanner skin than the Aryan
incels seething of fear make
believe invasions, infestations,
caravans coming...
that never arrive. Still
even on this side
of the border, in Mississippi,
you love showing your ilk
how to keep the darker shades
afraid of so many different Crayola
colors hiding con miedo. Do you
even understand
when niños y niñas cry

for their mami y papi?
What they mean? Do
you need to have
their copper cries whitewashed
in translation to bleach
away your conscience?
Why must you separate
our familias? Why focus
on us, the ones who speak
a marron lengua? I can
see you snicker while
laughing, always stepping on
our earth tones while
nose up admiring cloud
like colors, wishing
to whiteout America.
This must be why you
desire to "fix" the census,
we don't count, the only
families that matter
are the ones with $$$ —
green is the only color
you see. Anyone
of a darker shade, ruins the pale canvas
your vanilla American
wet dream. So, you cover
with silk, naturally blanketing
your sneers, never wanting
to hear our burnt umber cries—
forgetting all those niños
y niñas, in your eggshell
fragile mind—if you can't
see shiny seashell colors—
they're not your ivory children.

El Pasaporte es Mi Libertad?

Cuando manejo estoy buscando
luces rojas. I am often nervously
tenso, always imaginando the flashing

from la migra enforcement. I carry
mi Pasaporte porque no quiero
que me arresten por el color

de mi piel. Although soy
ciudadano legal, some with
badges son discriminatorio and only

see me as undocumented, a dreamer
target, wanting to lock me inside of
an ICE box, always ready to freeze—

manos arriba, no quiero escribir
pistola poesía. Mi proxima verso
titled: ¿Por qué tengo que explicar

que yo nací en Detroit? With so many
stuttering stanzas siempre feeling
attacked with more than mi ataques

de pánico, en mis manos is the only
shield for mi Inocencia. Mi pasaporte
es la única cosa I own that feels like

Libertad. Cuando camino around
mi barrio, mirando nerviosamente
for unlawful enforcement, I picture

them aiming for cualquiera que
parezca a mi. They are ready to handcuff
because I blush a lighter shade

of moreno. Con mi bilingual breaths
I am often hiperventilando, with
my face on concrete en la calle, as

they reach for my wallet, como tantos
que viven con angustia like me,
realizing because of the color of my

skin, en este país que Amo donde
nací, por que tengo que preguntar—
¿Todavía existo sin mi Pasaporte?

Las niñas have not disappeared

The ones ripped away
from the gripped loving

manos de los padres, now
taught a lesson, that this border

is no longer welcoming to the tired, sick
poor, no more smuggled masses

queriendo to breathe libertad
but they are greeted with chains

locked away incarceration.
The new American tearaway,

the liberty statue is now buried
deep in the sand and we are

Taylor at the end of *Planet of
the Apes*, fist on the beach

now gritando, *Que hiso, las
niñas no han desaparecido*

*you left them in cages, damn
you all to hell.* Distracted by

apps on your iPhone,
posing for selfies, scrolling

to see who Kardashian
is sexting… will you

remember the children
we ignored for over four años

still locked away frozen in chains
crying for Mami y Papi—

nunca recuredas, justified for
national insecurity, after all

this time forgotten forever, can
you remember these niñas are no threat.

"40 por ciento"

"This is the ritual for senseless death
to remove flowers and candles
[...] as if it never happened
reducing the value of life to nothingness"
                    —Jimmy Santiago Baca

En esta cuidad, no
queremos mas alas
de Los Angeles, somos
hijas, hijos, madres,
papas, abuelitos, abuelos
cada muerto apaga
la llama de la vida

"The experts claim not to know
our oppression [...] instead of
the real people we are [...]
their ideas replace us with
stereotypes that suit their
selfish needs," Jimmy sabe

no queremos celebrar
cumpleaños, no necesitamos
piñatas, no tenenmos sed
por botellas de tequilla
cuando estamos esperando
la llamada del hospital
o la morgue, con las manos
donde ganamos pequeños
centavos cavando la tierra
con nuestras propias tumbas—

"And when the fires of despair burn down
And darkness fills me
I [...] keep chopping my anger up
feeding it to the fire," Dígales Jimmy

el sueño de nuestra comunidad
queremos sobrevivir con salud,
sin miedo relajándose en paz
cuando vemos el dato: *40%*
de los muertos por Covid19
en Los Angeles son Latinos
mirando las noticas que otro
ha pasado a la *nothingness*
por qué no entienden que no
somos numeros, no todos
cantamos las mañanitas, no
vamos a estar silencio, llorando
a este país solamente gritamos
¡No más!

Gracias Amy Shimshon-Santo y Jimmy Santiago Baca

Invisible or Tan

Why do my neighbors and
my friends misunderstand
me? Speaking in mi lengua,
hablo con mi boca not with
my skin. Cuando camino in
shadows accenting borders,
I come from the land, mi voz
from la tierra. Hablo
con sueños demostrar
la pasión de mi lengua. Listen
to mi Corazon, beating
ritmos, sonriazs
but my Resistencia
resigns you. Always slighting
me, presume I exist
only as a gardener,
a niño immigrante. You
stranger call me stealer
dreamer, a child anchoring
alien illegal to your border,
separates me, your wall
another brick will erode
you, keeping your mind
blaming mi cuerpo, crumble
fall from the rumbling
of mi mente. Hear me singing,
calle marching unidos
con mis hermanas, hermanos,
familias, inciting canciones feel
me, soy hombre, I am man! —
my voice, mi fuerza,
hear my desire, oye

don't dare me to paint
me, rolling eyes over
my invisible tan—
when you are the ones
disappearing, whitewash
with emotions, reflecting
all that you hear, remember
recuerdo, soy hombre...
always, I will—
siempre withstand.

I am *Gentefied*

More than just mirando
otra programa en mi
television, when I watch

the Morales family, feels
more like an espejo,
a mirror into my own

lengua, mi corazon,
mis sueños, mis miedos,
el amor y cariño de mi

propio familia, lejos now
appears closer when I hear
the wisdom of Pop, Casimiro,

oigo consjeos de my own Papi.
Erik and Chris son como
mis hermanos, Ana was la

hermana que nunca tuve y
Lidia es la novia, nunca
salí con una sirena de

ensueño como ella—
when I watch, I cannot hold
back as tears aparecen en

mis ojos, seeing las calles
unidos con our fuerte gente
en Boyle Heights celebrando

our comunidad en la tele para
primera vez, for the first time
seeing a familia que habla,

pelea, que se quiren mucho,
y ellos comen la comedia that
Mama Fin has simmered

delicioso for years in our own
cocinas. From our loveseat,
watching con mi esposa, we

can taste los sabores. En cada
episodio, imagining the flavors,
por la primera vez mirando la tele,

I feel electrified seeing mi gente.
I love savoring the aroma, that
sabe como yo, radiante piel que

parece alguien que ama se ríe
y duele exactamente like me.

A Través del Espejo

recuerdo soaking from la ventana
driving causeway interstate
cliché gold pots despacio,
no camera era necesario
estoy viendo my own reflection
el sol, witnessing the glow—
even now when I blink
estático on the radio
salvación from some pastor
in the rust belt
but ahead, en el cielo
que vision—
I never saw a rainbow
like this—
a canvas of mirror
prisms
y finalmente veo
the open road
drenched in light.

This Is Not Just About Me

There is a weight of centuries
future, some past, withstanding
as my shoulders hunch over
on my back, but I will not
be buckling under mi miedo, watch
me rise, uplifting all those around
me and so many faceless others
watching me stumble behind
this microphone as my stutter
resounds imperfección, showing
all these would be dreamers
too late, nunca! If I can stand
here with my stammering,
what is stopping all of you?
This weight now feathers
as I watch my audience
become pájaros, ready to wing
their fears and just like me
birds overcome their shadows
gripping pens, paintbrushes,
cameras internally focusing while
shuddering fearless imaginación,
externally cielo, no limit while
watching their eyes soar instantly,
exploring clouds relentlessly,
becoming their gigantic fate.

Gracias Virginia Woolf

Cuando morimos

Our cuerpo turns into
poetry, skin lines
become typeface fonts
in stanzas eternally
wide, our spirit voices
no longer silent, now
rhyme on páginas
invisible, when spoken
aloud, we arise breaths
climaxing within las bocas
mouthing many volumes
reread, in the afterlife we
are more than remembered—
our body becomes
immortalized poesia.

Quienes son los enemigos?

It's the distributors, Jimmy Santiago.
I tried ordering *No Enemies* from your
publisher and they canceled my order.

Even though su libro was 'officially"
released, there were no copies for me to buy.
How can a legendary Poeta have a new

book out that no one puede comprar?
Sandra Cisneros me dijo, *Latinos are
the illegal aliens de la industria publishing.*

So many of us on las líneas del frente,
wielding our pluma swords inking la
sangra en las paginas that many no

quiere publicar, sell, distribute or want
us to read. They try to silence us but
nosotros seguimos escribiendo poema

after poema, our unheard voz resounding
louder on every stanza. Still some are
nourishing our palabras, estamos cantando

con Flower Song Press, Edward Vidaurre
is harnessing and publishing volumes
of so many poetas LatinX, Alegria, y

Davina A. Ferreira en Los Angeles esta
tambien building a movement of escritores
with our words, our lengua, our voces.

Despite problemas con distribution our
libros are being seen, shared, gifted,
so many who speak like us are leyendo

our poemas. We sell, so many quieren
leer our stories, nuestras verses, ellos
dicen, estos libros ring like la vida. So

many the tired of same whitewash cliché
privileged pages. Muchas en nuestra
comunidad quieren books that speak

to them in their own beautifully lengua
fuerte in libros they are ready to own.
Damn the distribution, Jimmy Santiago,

yo finalmente tengo *No Enemies* in mis
manos, mis hermanas y hermanos poetas
feed on your callings, crafted poemas

politicos not just for our purchasing
power, our demographic are wanting
mas libros from our lengua, desde

nuestra experiencias, a colección de
poesía like yours inspires so many,
each page is an espejo tan poderosa,

una pagina can create una revolucionaria
by leyendo palabras, novelas, stories y
poemas. Despite those distributors, we are no longer

daydreaming, nosotros estamos escribiendo
on our MacBook's, writing using papel to
soñar in notebook journals, filming our

verses on YouTube, TikTok and on Insta Stories. We are
already content creating, our own volúmenes
read louder from the bookshelf along with

Baca, Cisneros, Espada, Neruda, Urrea, Cepeda,
Luis J. Rodriguez, Gris Muñoz, Jenn Givhan,
Ada Limón, Alma Luz Villanueva, Briana

Muñoz, Sonia Gutiérrez, Angelina Sáenz,
Erika L. Sánchez, Juan Felipe Herrera,
Natalie Diaz, Alberto Ríos, José Olivarez,

Iris De Anda, Gina Duran, Eloisa Amezcua,
Natalie Garcia, Javier Zamora, Matt Sedillo,
David A. Romero, Natalie Sierra, Luivette Resto,

Leslie Contreras Schwartz, Fernando Albert
Salinas, Jose Hernandez Diaz, Ariel Francisco,
Steven Alvarez, Julio Serrano Echeverría, Roberto

Carlos Garcia, Leticia Urieta, César L. de León,
Jean-Pierre Rueda, Jesenia Chávez, Virginia
Bulacio, Paul S. Flores, Margaret Elysia Garcia,

Ceasar K. Avelar, Donato Martinez, Anatalia
Vallez, ire'ne lara silva, Xochitl-Julisa Bermejo—
our LatinX literatura legacy, to those

unpublished dreamers, envision picturing your
own book, the cover of our futuro, su libro will
un día proudly glow brillante in nuestras casas.

Pilgrimage from San Antonio to Corpus Christi

We called out sick—
enfermo for her. We left
la cuidad del Alamo racing

away from Borders, la librería
where nosotros cuatro worked.
Even before we packed up in my

verde Mazda 626, as I signaled
onto I-37 Sur, we heard her distant
voice calling us, coming from

my car stereo… *Ven Conmigo*
spinning in my CD player
ventanas roll, peregrinaje volumes

turned up when she sang,
Ven conmigo, quiero hacerte
mi Tesoro. I wanted to be

the treasure, she was singing
her serenata, to. We all joined
todos, on repeat, spinning

the same canción that carried
us all dos horas to Corpus
and when we arrived at Mirador

de la Flor, as the waves of
the Gulf were trying to splash
away our tears, standing

delante de Selena's statue
we could no longer sing.
As we joined manos, we waited

for her preciosa voz from
la estatua, overlooking her
flower, to wash away

our tristeza and sing in
a circle, hoping with each
lírica nosotros podríamos

pausar el tiempo but time
would not stop. As el sol sunk
into the Gulf our signal

to jump back in mi Mazda
where her musica was waiting
for us, turning up el volume

fuerte, ready for la
canción to carry us all
the way on our viaje largo

back home where we did not
belong, but, before we left,
I had to drop to one knee saying

one final prayer to her espíritu—
Selena, let us vivir con sus
palabras, as we drove away,

soñamos, con our promesa
siempre recordaremos el día
on our pilgrimage, we pledged

inside all her corazón of songs
that leave us choked—we evoke
our tears.

Why LA?

When others ask me,
I tell them my life
was pulled by
our tectonic plates,
the force of mi vida
gravitational called
me here, the LA Glow
reverberating vibrantly
so much sun, puffy
cielo cloudy bright
azul skies welcoming
me, my city motor eyes.
No era sopresa,
along with my once reluctant
wallflower stuttering
mouth, I found, my voz
no longer feared
my stammering—
I was becoming
every day embracing
Brian Wilson, Luis J. Rodriguez
Robin Coste Lewis, Amanda
Gorman, reopening Morrison's
Doors, exploring Bukowski,
Didion, Babitz Eve, Francesca
Lia Block, Kerouac's
passageways opened
my calling, I answered—
finally, when microphones
ask me in between flashes—
I sonrisa grin and say—
Not just mi casa, my home,

roaming no longer soñando
California, cuando encontré
mi cuidad de Angeles,
I discovered myself—
inside my poems.

Neruda is ▮▮▮▮▮▮▮▮ **Spanish** ▮▮

▮ The Heights of ▮▮▮▮▮ his ▮▮ poem ▮ made ▮▮▮▮
▮▮▮▮▮▮▮▮▮▮▮ *amor* ▮▮▮▮▮▮▮▮▮▮
▮▮▮▮▮▮ ▮▮▮▮▮▮▮ in ▮ Spanish ▮
alone— ▮▮▮▮▮▮▮▮▮▮▮▮▮▮▮▮
▮▮▮▮▮▮▮▮▮▮▮ his ▮▮▮▮▮▮▮▮
▮▮▮▮ real name ▮▮▮▮▮▮▮▮▮▮
▮▮▮▮▮▮▮▮ coined ▮▮▮▮ the exotic ▮▮▮ of ▮
▮▮▮▮▮▮▮▮▮▮▮▮▮ "Pablo." His early ▮▮▮
▮▮▮▮▮▮▮▮▮▮▮▮▮▮▮▮▮
Poemas ▮▮ gained ▮▮▮▮▮▮▮▮ a close-knit ▮▮
▮▮ symbolism to define ▮▮▮▮ his personal ▮▮▮ experience.

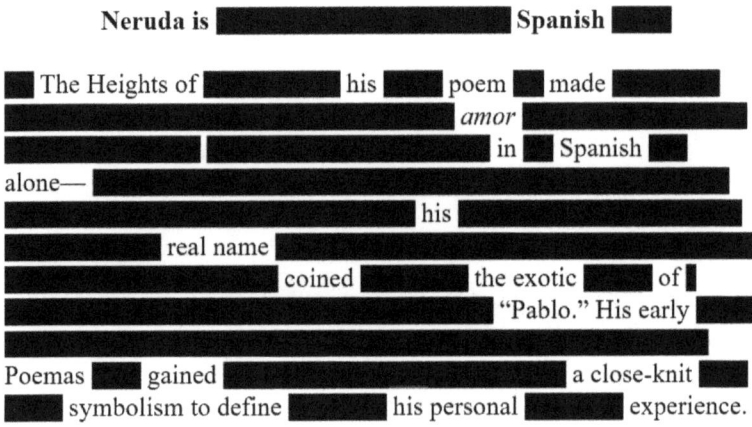

from **Robert <u>Pring</u>-Mill's** Preface in **Pablo Neruda's** *The Heights of Macchu Picchu*

I was in total silencio until

opening Ginsberg, Allen
taught me to *Howl* using
every bit of mi garganta.

I was no longer afraid of taking
the chapter, riding on the road,
en este camino, Kerouac

urging me to leap inside
my own página, use mi
lengua, enunciating my own

mañana, seducing palabras
with my tongue. Ferlinghetti
loves telling me poesia is

my lover desnuda, between
our labios, kissing the distance
between the spine, we love taking

turns tonguing Burroughs lines,
making out with *Naked Lunch*,
always leaves me hungering

for City Lights, following
my own rhythm, San Francisco
causing tremors, stammering

forward, the wheels driving
me to journey towards the horizon—
reflecting my own shadow,

scribbling outside highway
lines, becoming verses within
each curve, calling Big Sur—

as my feet splashing on my own
private beach, driving within
the waves, embracing desolation

angels telling me listen to su
Corazon. Now when I reignite
Poesia from my mouth, no longer

fear the stuttering aftershocks,
each beat sparked me to no longer
be silent, like Kerouac in front

of the transistor, I am now
cranking my Español volume,
turning on mi vida writing

while exploring on the page—
hear me bailando bilingual,
dancing to the Gemini

voice of my own speaker ritmo,
feel me proudly— Howling aloud.

I Know This is Muy Dificil

"Breathe Keep breathing I can't do this Alone"
—Thomas Edward Yorke

Keep exhaling. Let the pen
marker black, scratch out
words. Let the page be your
voz. With each erasure
mi compañera tu siempre
star… recreating breaths,
clouds once flowing out
with poetry are now polluting
trapped inside your lungs—
these pulmonary poemas
keep grasping with each
gripping of your pluma—
su boca resilient, sus labios
can feel these creation gusts
coming, expanding pulmón
pulsating inside, forget la tos,
each cough another line
break, don't fear the next
wheezing gust, immortalize
yourself on paper, press
save and remember mi amiga
every rhyme you have
ever uttered will echo then
resound, expanding, you
are la aire, respirar su poesia—
no more thoughts of pecho
dolor, you will sobrevivir.
From here I can feel you inhaling
words and exhaling poems,

with each stanza, I know
this is muy dificil, you
withstand while outlasting
each gasp, debes exhalar
e inhalar por la nariz—
more than envision, mi
hermana you will feel
la voz de mañana ready to
reignite triumphantly proud.

Poetry Journey

Cento poem from Pablo Neruda's: The Complete Memoirs

Walking against
sealed wombs aware
of the burn, my words
journey, companion you
to recognize my poetry—
she, my guide dark
flare driven love
suffusing of solitudes,
today, my voice accepts
you, wounded, sometimes
cheer, as this unchained forest
shatters, my secret heart
lights deep in tenderness,
gulfs flames age of lost
love, the mother of
my solitudes, discovery
of thorns in depths,
my anxiety sea grasps
dark wind, impassioned
flight blaze in echoes,
the joy of poetry nets—
my pleasures of night.

Somos Espejos

The glass where you
appear, every morning
after showering, en
el baño, toweling

off all that you fear—
the mirror we are,
from our being,
every cell that flashes—

exposing cada selfie,
we float into the clouds
a virtual photo album
that we click to share

and revisit, eternally
for years, we are
mirroring

recuredos
de madres,
y abuelitas,

recalling their
voices en la mañana—
louder yelling us
downstairs to our

cuartos in la noche—
so many consejos
still ringing you always
loved to ear. You can

feel their accents,
the same one who
sweetly held us from
first breath until we

grip their wrinkling
hands, unable to pause
the hourglass sands before

they quietly disappeared.
The mirror we are,
the faces we shared

sticking our lenguas
of laughter with
sisters, hermanos,
tías and uncles

who return with
flashes of alegría,
simmering with Domingo
barbacoa, quesadillas,

the holiest of guacamoles
we still savor in our
bocas tan ricas, deliciously
drunk in remembrances—

we reimagine still
tasting unbottling tequilas,
cervezas after so many

años and tears, we are
your mirror, illuminating
a renewed reawakening—

clearly these words
you hear so familiar
ageless in wonder,
no matter our birthplace

we resound so much closer,
within this glass, somos espejos,
reflecting sonriente blessed—
you love to reappear.

About the Author

Adrian Ernesto Cepeda is the author of *Flashes & Verses…
Becoming Attractions* from Unsolicited Press, *Between the Spine*
from Picture Show Press, *Speaking con su Sombra* with Alegría
Publishing, *La Belle Ajar* & *We Are the Ones Possessed* from
CLASH Books and his 6th poetry collection *La Lengua Inside
Me* is published with FlowerSong Press.

Adrian lives with his wife in Los Angeles with their adorably
spoiled cat Woody Gold.

FLOWERSONG
P R E S S

FlowerSong Press nurtures essential verse
from, about, and throughout the
borderlands. Literary. Lyrical. Boundless.

Sign up for announcements about
new and upcoming titles at:

www.flowersongpress.com

www.ingramcontent.com/pod-product-compliance
Lightning Source LLC
Chambersburg PA
CBHW051526120626
46551CB00012B/1099